W9-CBU-312

HomeBuilders *Couples Series* ®

resolving

Conflict
in Your Marriage

By Bob and Jan Horner

*"Unless the Lord
builds the house,
its builders
labor in vain"*
(Psalm 127:1a).

FAMILYLIFE™
Bringing Timeless Principles Home
Little Rock, Arkansas

Group
Loveland, Colorado

Group's R.E.A.L. Guarantee® to you:

This Group resource incorporates our R.E.A.L. approach to ministry—one that encourages long-term retention and life transformation. It's ministry that's:

Relational
Because learner-to-learner interaction enhances learning and builds Christian friendships.

Experiential
Because what learners experience through discussion and action sticks with them up to 9 times longer than what they simply hear or read.

Applicable
Because the aim of Christian education is to equip learners to be both hearers and doers of God's Word.

Learner-based
Because learners understand and retain more when the learning process takes into consideration how they learn best.

Visit our Web site: **www.grouppublishing.com**

Credits
FamilyLife
Editor: David Boehi
Assistant Editor: Julie Denker

Group Publishing, Inc.
Editor: Matt Lockhart
Creative Development Editor: Paul Woods
Chief Creative Officer: Joani Schultz
Copy Editor: Bob Kretschman
Art Director: Jenette L. McEntire
Cover Art Director: Jeff A. Storm
Computer Graphic Artist: Anita M. Cook
Cover Photographer: FPG International
Illustrator: Ken Jacobsen
Production Manager: Peggy Naylor

Unless otherwise noted, Scripture taken from the HOLY BIBLE, NEW INTERNATIONAL VERSION®. Copyright © 1973, 1978, 1984 by International Bible Society. Used by permission of Zondervan Publishing House. All rights reserved.

ISBN 0-7644-2240-5
18 17 16 15 14 13 12 11 10 9 8   09 08 07 06 05 04

Printed in the United States of America.

How to Let the Lord Build Your House
and not labor in vain

●

The HomeBuilders Couples Series®: A small-group Bible study dedicated to making your family all that God intended.

FamilyLife is a division of Campus Crusade for Christ International, an evangelical Christian organization founded in 1951 by Bill Bright. FamilyLife was started in 1976 to help fulfill the Great Commission by strengthening marriages and families and then equipping them to go to the world with the gospel of Jesus Christ. The FamilyLife Marriage Conference is held in most major cities throughout the United States and is one of the fastest-growing marriage conferences in America today. "FamilyLife Today," a daily radio program hosted by Dennis Rainey, is heard on hundreds of stations across the country. Information on all resources offered by FamilyLife may be obtained by contacting us at the address, telephone number, or World Wide Web site listed below.

Dennis Rainey, Executive Director
FamilyLife
P.O. Box 8220
Little Rock, AR 72221-8220
1-800-FL-TODAY
www.familylife.com

A division of Campus Crusade for Christ International
Bill Bright, Founder and President

112303

About the Sessions

Each session in this study is composed of the following categories: Warm-Up, Blueprints, Wrap-Up, and HomeBuilders Project. A description of each of these categories follows:

Warm-Up (15 minutes)

The purpose of Warm-Up is to help people unwind from a busy day and get to know each other better. Typically the first point in Warm-Up is an exercise that is meant to be fun while introducing the topic of the session. The ability to share in fun with others is important in building relationships. Another component of Warm-Up is the Project Report (except in Session One), which is designed to provide accountability for the HomeBuilders Project that is to be completed by couples between sessions.

Blueprints (60 minutes)

This is the heart of the study. In this part of each session, people answer questions related to the topic of study and look to God's Word for understanding. Some of the questions are to be answered by couples, in subgroups, or in the group at large. There are notes in the margin or instructions within a question that designate these groupings.

Wrap-Up (15 minutes)

 This category serves to "bring home the point" and wind down a session in an appropriate fashion.

HomeBuilders Project (60 minutes)

 This project is the unique application step in a HomeBuilders study. Before leaving a meeting, couples are encouraged to "Make a Date" to do this project prior to the next meeting. Each HomeBuilders Project contains three sections: 1) As a Couple—a brief exercise designed to get the date started in a fun way; 2) Individually—a section of questions for husbands and wives to answer separately; 3) Interact as a Couple—an opportunity for couples to share their answers with each other and to make application in their lives.

In addition to the above regular features, occasional activities are labeled "For Extra Impact." These are activities that generally provide a more active or visual way to make a particular point. Be mindful that people within a group have different learning styles. While most of what is presented is verbal, a visual or active exercise now and then helps engage more of the senses and appeals to people who learn best by seeing, touching, and doing.

About the Authors

Bob and Jan Horner have long been co-workers—as partners in marriage, parents of three daughters, staff members of Campus Crusade for Christ International, and speakers at FamilyLife Marriage Conferences.

Bob is a graduate of Westmont College and the University of Colorado with a degree in mechanical engineering. He joined the staff of Campus Crusade in 1964. Jan became part of Campus Crusade two years later, after finishing her education at Colorado State University. They work with Campus Crusade's Marketplace Connections, equipping graduating university students to enter the world of work with confident workplace ministry skills. Bob has also co-authored three books for Promise Keepers with his colleague, David Sunde, including *Applying the Seven Promises.*

Bob and Jan continue to invest much of their time and energy in addressing the needs of couples and families. They are part of a growing number of couples who speak at FamilyLife Marriage Conferences around the world. Bob and Jan have the great privilege of equipping these couples to effectively present God's principles for marriage.

Their three daughters, Kelley, Shawna, and Andrea, are now grown and gone from their home in Boulder, Colorado. Now the Horner household is becoming the welcome spot for sons-in-law, grandchildren, and...well, more opportunities to resolve conflict.

Contents

Acknowledgments

There is a Book that gives hope. It is "profitable for teaching, for reproof, for correction, for training in righteousness; that the man [and woman] of God may be adequate, equipped for every good work" (2 Timothy 3:16-17, New American Standard Bible). Certainly marriage is a "good work." We are grateful to the One who inspired the Bible, and to his Son, for providing the basis for resolving all conflict.

Campus Crusade for Christ has provided the nurturing environment needed for our thirty-two years of marriage. We have been given vision for our lives, time to grow up, training, help in raising our three children, and the privilege of working among the finest associates possible. You have helped us to know and love the Author of marriage.

The Merediths, founders of FamilyLife, were the first to give us workable solutions to conflicts we discovered in our marriage. Don and Sally, thank you for the friendship!

Dennis and Barbara Rainey are not only the visionaries behind the HomeBuilders Couples Series and thus this study, but favorite friends and co-workers who have "pushed" us into speaking and writing with FamilyLife. Thanks for the loving shove, you two!

Ideas and concepts need the shaping of craftsmen. Julie Denker and Dave Boehi, you have chiseled and sanded and polished our work into something to which we are proud to give our signature. We have told you more than once, and we say it again, "You are geniuses!"

To the many groups around the country who first piloted this project...thanks for the feedback. Your input was invaluable. You will likely see those contributions as you use this study again.

There really is nothing new under the sun. This study has evolved out of learning from favorite authors such as Paul Tournier, James Dobson, Gary Smalley, H. Norman Wright, Ed Wheat, and Willard F. Harley, Jr., and from some of our favorite people who work alongside us as fellow speakers with FamilyLife.

Foreword

Conflict is a common denominator of every marriage. No relationship is free from the friction caused by our differences and expectations—and by our just being human. Repeatedly this subject is mentioned by our FamilyLife Marriage Conference guests as one of the most critical issues they face in their marriages. Yet few have received the training they need to know how to successfully handle the hurt, misunderstandings, and difficulties encountered in a normal marriage relationship.

That's why I asked Bob and Jan Horner to tackle this thorny problem—to equip you with practical "how-to's" for resolving conflict between husband and wife. As staff members with Campus Crusade for Christ, the Horners have teamed up to enrich the lives of college students and lay couples all around the world. Since 1982, they have spoken to thousands annually as speakers at our FamilyLife Marriage Conference.

You'll find that Bob and Jan have blended together strong biblical principles with practical questions and projects that will challenge you to change the way you think about conflict. The Horners are in touch with the needs of couples and individuals today, and I am confident that their study will encourage you to dig to new and deeper levels of communication as husband and wife.

Dennis Rainey

Executive Director, FamilyLife

Introduction

When a man and woman are married, they stand before a room of witnesses and proclaim their commitment to a lifetime of love. They recite a sacred vow "to have and to hold...from this day forward...to love, honor, and cherish...for better, for worse...for richer, for poorer...in sickness and in health...as long as we both shall live."

It's a happy day, perhaps the happiest in their lives. And yet, once the honeymoon ends, once the emotions of courtship and engagement subside, many couples realize that "falling in love" and building a good marriage are two different things. Keeping those vows is much more difficult than they thought it would be.

Otherwise intelligent people, who would not think of buying a car, investing money, or even going to the grocery store without some initial planning, enter into marriage with no plan of how to make that relationship succeed.

But God has already provided the plan, a set of blueprints for building a truly God-honoring marriage. His plan is designed to enable a man and woman to grow together in a mutually satisfying relationship and then to reach out to others with the love of Christ. Ignoring this plan leads only to isolation and separation between husband and wife. It's a pattern evident in so many homes today: Failure to follow God's blueprints results in wasted effort, bitter disappointment, and, in far too many cases, divorce.

In response to this need in marriages today, FamilyLife has developed a series of small-group studies called the HomeBuilders Couples Series.

You could complete this study alone with your spouse, but we strongly urge you to either form or join a group of couples studying this material. You will find that the questions in each session not only help you grow closer to your spouse, but they help create a special environment of warmth and fellowship as you study together how to build the type of marriage you desire. Participating in a HomeBuilders group could be one of the highlights of your married life.

The Bible: Your Blueprints for a God-Honoring Marriage

You will notice as you proceed through this study that the Bible is used frequently as the final authority on issues of life and marriage. Although written thousands of years ago, this Book still speaks clearly and powerfully about the conflicts and struggles faced by men and women. The Bible is God's Word— his blueprints for building a God-honoring home and for dealing with the practical issues of living.

We encourage you to have a Bible with you for each session. For this series we use the New International Version as our primary reference. Another excellent translation is the New American Standard Bible.

Ground Rules

Each group session is designed to be enjoyable and informative—and nonthreatening. Three simple ground rules will help ensure that everyone feels comfortable and gets the most out of the experience:

1. Don't share anything that would embarrass your spouse.

2. You may pass on any question you don't want to answer.

3. If possible, plan to complete the HomeBuilders Project as a couple between group sessions.

A Few Quick Notes About Leading a HomeBuilders Group

1. Leading a group is much easier than you may think! A group leader in a HomeBuilders session is really a "facilitator." As a leader, your goal is simply to guide the group through the discussion questions. You don't need to teach the material—in fact, we don't want you to! The special dynamic of a HomeBuilders group is that couples teach themselves.

2. This material is designed to be used in a home study, but it also can be adapted for use in a Sunday school environment. (See page 105 for more information about this option.)

3. We have included a section of Leader's Notes in the back of this book. Be sure to read through these notes before leading a session; they will help you prepare.

4. For more material on leading a HomeBuilders group, get a copy of the *HomeBuilders Leader Guide*, by Drew and Kit Coons. This book is an excellent resource that provides helpful guidelines on how to start a study, how to keep discussion moving, and much more.

A Word About Resolving Conflict

Conflict is inevitable. The difference between any two couples is not whether there is conflict, but what the partners do with it when it surfaces. *Resolving Conflict in Your Marriage* has been prepared for husbands and wives who wish to have their conflicts produce greater communication and understanding within marriage.

As a couple, you will not be required to relate your personal conflicts within the group. However, you will be encouraged to uncover, discuss, and resolve those conflicts alone as a couple. This study surfaces issues that many couples have carefully suppressed or have purposely ignored. Defusing these "time bombs" is difficult, but oh, so necessary; therefore, don't be surprised if it seems you are experiencing greater conflict during this study than before you began. It is all part of learning the joy that comes with communication and understanding.

We commend you for investing in your marriage by rolling up your sleeves and digging into what is so important to you and the generations that will follow you—resolving conflict in marriage.

Bob and Jan Horner

Recognizing Conflict

God's design for marriage leads to a meaningful and valued relationship between husband and wife. Since conflict is inevitable in marriage, we must discover how to use it in building this relationship through communication and understanding.

W A R M • U P   15   M I N U T E S

After couples introduce themselves, take a minute to individually complete the following exercise.

Viva la Différence!

For each of the following categories, decide whether you and your spouse are more similar or different. For each item, circle either S (representing "similar") or D (representing "different").

Personality	**S**	**D**
Sense of humor	**S**	**D**
Musical tastes	**S**	**D**
Family background	**S**	**D**
Special interests	**S**	**D**

After completing this exercise, compare results with your spouse, and then answer these questions as a group:

- Who had the most number of items marked as similar? different?
- What are some ways that differences between a husband and wife might strengthen a marriage?
- Discuss together the importance of recognizing differences in dealing with conflict.

Getting Connected

Pass your books around the room, and have each couple write their names, phone numbers, and e-mail addresses.

NAME, PHONE, & E-MAIL

NAME, PHONE, & E-MAIL

NAME, PHONE, & E-MAIL

NAME, PHONE, & E-MAIL

NAME, PHONE, & E-MAIL

NAME, PHONE, & E-MAIL

Marriage is an attempt to blend together two distinctly different individuals—a man and a woman who have different backgrounds, values, and personalities. Is it any wonder that conflict exists in marriage?

Understanding Conflict

1. Many factors can produce conflict in marriage. One of these is personality differences (for example, emotional vs. reserved). What are some ways that personality differences can cause strife in marriage?

If you have a large group, form smaller groups of about six people to answer the Blueprints questions. Unless otherwise noted, answer the questions in your subgroup. After finishing each section, take time for subgroups to relate their answers with the whole group.

2. Different values and philosophies is another area of potential disagreement. What are some issues that couples often have different views on? What might be some of the problems associated with the issues you've identified?

3. Additionally, men and women have basic differences.

- *Men:* What are some things that men typically find difficult to understand about women? What do you believe are some misunderstandings that women sometimes have about men?

- *Women:* What do women typically find difficult to understand about men? What do you believe are some ways that men sometimes misunderstand women?

HomeBuilders Principle:
Understanding and valuing differences between you and your spouse is the first step toward resolving conflict.

The Impact of Conflict

4. Read Ephesians 4:26-27.

- When does anger become sin?

- What do you think it means to "not let the sun go down while you are still angry"?

5. What effect does unresolved conflict have on a relationship? How might this "give the devil a foothold"?

6. What do you remember learning from your parents about handling conflict—good or bad?

7. What are some common sources of conflict in your marriage?

Answer questions 7 and 8 with your spouse. After answering, you may want to share an appropriate insight or discovery with the group.

8. What effect has unresolved conflict had on your marriage?

HomeBuilders Principle:
Unresolved conflict hurts your marriage.

Pursuing Peace

Although conflict occurs, it is not God's ideal. God desires that we experience peace and unity in marriage.

9. The Bible has much to say about peace. Each couple should look up one of the following Scriptures. (Depending on the number of people in your group, it's OK for a couple to look up more than one passage or for more than one couple to look up the same passage.)

- Psalm 34:12-14
- Isaiah 26:3
- Romans 12:17-18
- Romans 14:17-19
- Colossians 3:15
- Hebrews 12:14

Read your passage and discuss what it says about peace. Then read your passage to the group and tell how it relates to living in peace.

10. Read John 14:27. How is what Jesus offers different from what the world gives?

11. According to the following verses, how can we experience the peace of God?

- Romans 5:1

- Colossians 1:19-20

- Ephesians 2:14-16

12. In achieving lasting peace in marriage, what advantage, do Christians have over non-Christians?

HomeBuilders Principle:
A peaceful relationship with your spouse is possible when you pursue God's peace in your life.

W R A P • U P   15   M I N U T E S

In this session, you discussed understanding conflict and pursuing peace. Now it's time to move into action—to practice pursuing peace! From the following list, individually select the situation that would most bother you. After

After you complete the Wrap-Up activity, close this session with prayer, and make sure couples Make a Date for this session's HomeBuilders Project before they leave.

you make your selection, get with your spouse and discuss how to deal with the situation. After you finish, share with the group one of your situations and how you decided to deal with the conflict.

Bothersome Behaviors

- You find yourself continually changing the thermostat because your spouse sets it "too hot" or "too cold."

- You leave the house running late for an appointment and discover that the gas gauge of your car is on "empty." (Oh, and your seat is in the wrong position, and all your radio-station settings have been changed.)

- The phone bill is higher than you think it should be. Someone is using it for more than agreed upon.

- You just received a bank statement indicating four $25 charges for overdrawing your checking account.

- Guests have been invited over for dinner without your knowledge.

Make a Date

Make a date with your spouse to meet before the next session to complete the HomeBuilders Project. Your leader will ask at the next session for you to share one thing from this experience.

HOMEBUILDERS PROJECT   6 0   M I N U T E S

As a Couple [10 minutes]

To start your date, talk together about an experience you had growing up with a bully or someone you just couldn't seem to get along with. After relating your experiences, discuss these questions:

- As a child, what were you taught, and by whom, about how to deal with people you had trouble getting along with?

- If you have children or plan to, what have you taught them, or plan to teach them, about how to deal with a bully?

Individually [20 minutes]

1. What is one thing you have learned from Session One that you want to apply?

2. When conflicts arise in your marriage, how do they generally affect you?

3. Thinking about how you and your spouse relate to each other, how would you rate your effectiveness in handling conflict? Circle the number on the following scale that you think most applies.

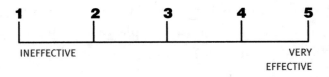

1   2   3   4   5

INEFFECTIVE   VERY
                              EFFECTIVE

4. What effect—positive and negative—would you say conflict has had on your marriage?

5. What is one thing you appreciate about how your spouse handles conflict in your marriage?

6. If you could change one thing about how you handle conflict, what it would be?

7. What do you hope to gain from the rest of this Home-Builders study?

Interact as a Couple [30 minutes]

1. Talk together about your answers from the previous section. *Note:* Resolve ahead of time that you will not argue! And try to be open, kind, and understanding as you address sensitive areas.

2. Discuss one or two currently unresolved conflicts between you, and how you might be able to deal with them.

3. Read the verses from the Blueprints question 9 from this session (page 20). What is one aspect of peace that these verses mention that you would like to see more of in your marriage?

4. Take a minute to pray together that God can use this study to help strengthen your marriage.

Remember to take your calendar to the next session so you can Make a Date.

Transparency

Resolving conflict in marriage requires transparency between you and your spouse.

W A R M • U P   15   M I N U T E S

Something Between Us

Each couple should have an item representing a communication filter. Turn to your spouse, and talk with each other about the kind of day you've had today. However, as you talk, be sure you hold up the filter between you. After everyone has experienced the different filters, discuss the following questions:

Leader: For further instructions and supplies that you need for this exercise, refer to the Leader's Notes for this session (p. 114).

- How did it feel to have the various communication filters between you as you talked?

- What difference did the type of filter that was between you make in the way that you communicated?

- What are some not-so-visible filters that can affect the transparency between couples?

Project Report

Tell of one thing you learned from the last session's HomeBuilders Project.

BLUEPRINTS 60 MINUTES

Being transparent—*real*—with your spouse is a key ingredient in a healthy marriage. Being transparent is risky, but the rewards are great. Transparency leads to deeper trust and intimacy in a relationship.

The Need for Transparency

"No one comes to know himself through introspection, or in the solitude of his personal diary. He who would see himself clearly must open up to a confidant freely chosen and worthy of trust."

Dr. Paul Tournier, psychiatrist

1. When you hear the word "transparency," what are some other words that come to mind? How can these words, when applied to marriage, be helpful?

If you have a large group, form smaller groups of about six people to answer the Blueprints questions. Unless otherwise noted, answer the questions in your subgroup. After finishing each section, take time for subgroups to relate their answers with the whole group.

2. Why is it often difficult to be transparent with others, even those who are closest to us?

3. Most people marry with the hope of being transparent, of openly sharing their thoughts and feelings with each other. In what ways is this hope of transparency damaged in many relationships? Why do couples feel the need for transparency in marriage?

4. Your spouse probably knows you better than anyone does. Tell each other what you like about this by completing the following sentence: The best part of being known so well by you is...

Answer questions 4 and 5 with your spouse. After you answer, you may want to share an appropriate insight or discovery with the group.

5. What is difficult for you about your spouse knowing you so well? Complete this sentence: Being known so well by you is difficult for me because...

Four Steps Toward Transparency

Step One: *Be open with God.*
Read Psalm 139:23-24.

6. King David was open with God. Do you find this type of transparency with God difficult or easy? Why?

Step Two: *Create an atmosphere of love, commitment, and forgiveness in your home.*
Read Colossians 3:12-14.

7. In what ways do you find creating this type of atmosphere to be difficult? easy?

Step Three: *Affirm your spouse when he or she practices transparency.*
Read Proverbs 16:24.

8. Why is it important to acknowledge and praise your spouse's efforts to be honest and transparent with you?

Step Four: *Pray regularly with one another.*
Read Colossians 4:2.

9. In what ways can open and honest prayer together promote transparency and intimacy?

HomeBuilders Principle:
An environment of love, commitment, and forgiveness encourages a person's willingness to be known by another.

Stifling Transparency

Case Study

Anne is having trouble with her mother-in-law. Anne tries to talk to her husband, Bill, about her problem. "Bill, I'm really struggling with the way your mother treats me. Whenever she visits, she tries to rearrange the kitchen. And she always has a better way to do whatever I'm doing." Bill, interrupting, responds, "It's not that big of a deal. You *know* how she can be."

10. What has Bill done to stifle Anne's attempt to be transparent with him?

11. If Bill were more transparent with Anne, what is a more appropriate response that he could have given?

12. Each couple should pick at least one of the following verses, read the Scripture, and discuss with each other what counsel this passage offers you as you seek to be more transparent with your spouse. Then read your verse and relate your insights to the group.

- Proverbs 10:19
- Proverbs 12:18
- Proverbs 13:3
- Proverbs 15:23
- Proverbs 25:11
- James 3:5

HomeBuilders Principle:
To enjoy the privileges of transparency, the power of the tongue must be used wisely.

W R A P • U P   15   M I N U T E S

In closing, review the Four Steps Toward Transparency:

Step One: *Be open with God.*

Step Two: *Create an atmosphere of love, commitment, and forgiveness in your home.*

Step Three: *Affirm your spouse when he or she practices transparency.*

Step Four: *Pray regularly with one another.*

- As a group, review Step One by discussing some practical ways that you can be open with God. What have you found to be helpful?

- To review Steps Two and Three, turn to your spouse and discuss ways you can create an atmosphere that promotes greater transparency between you; then talk about ways you can affirm each other, or talk about a time when your spouse was transparent with you that you really appreciated.

- Practice Step Four by making plans to pray together at least three times this next week. Pray with each other now that God would help you to be transparent with him and with your spouse.

Make a Date

Make a date with your spouse to meet before the next session to complete the HomeBuilders Project. Your leader will ask at the next session for you to share one thing from this experience.

_____
DATE

_____
TIME

_____
LOCATION

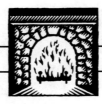

HOMEBUILDERS PROJECT　　　　　　　　**6 0   M I N U T E S**

As a Couple [10 minutes]

How well do you really know your spouse? Take the following quiz and find out!

Complete the following sentences:

My spouse's favorite color is...

My spouse's favorite TV show is...

My spouse's favorite movie is...

My spouse's favorite book is...

My spouse's favorite flavor of ice cream is...

My spouse's favorite store is...

My spouse's favorite room in the house is...

My spouse's favorite time of the day is...

My spouse's favorite season of the year is...

My spouse's favorite vacation spot is...

My spouse's favorite radio station is...

After you answer these questions, share your answers. How did you do? Now answer this question:

- What can you do to help your spouse know you better?

Individually [20 minutes]

Communication takes place in varying degrees of openness. The following descriptions show where transparency fits in the communication continuum. All of these levels of communication are used to some extent in every marriage. (Adapted from *Why Am I Afraid to Tell You Who I Am?* by John Powell)

Level One: **Cliché** communication allows a person to remain safely isolated and alone. Cliché communication consists of greetings and comments that express no opinions, feelings, or real information.

Level Two: **Fact** communication consists only of the objective discussion of facts. Data analysis holds others at arm's length.

Level Three: **Opinion** communication involves sharing ideas and opinions that open a person up.

Level Four: **Emotional** communication involves sharing feelings and emotions that lead to true communication. Emotional communication conveys a person's hopes, fears, likes, dislikes, aspirations, disappointments, joys, sorrows, needs, dreams, failures, desires, stresses, sources of fulfillment, discouragements, and burdens.

Level Five: **Transparent** communication involves complete emotional and personal truthfulness. Transparency is sharing your heart.

1. Evaluate how effectively you communicate with your spouse in the various levels of communication. In the following chart, assign a letter grade (A, B, C, D, or F) that you believe best rates your communication at each level.

Communication level	Meaning	Grade
Cliché	No sharing	
Fact	Sharing what you know	
Opinion	Sharing what you think	
Emotional	Sharing what you feel	
Transparent	Sharing who you are	

2. What might be one step you could take to move toward greater transparency?

3. Now evaluate how well you think your spouse communicates in each area.

Communication level	Meaning	Grade
Cliché	No sharing	
Fact	Sharing what you know	
Opinion	Sharing what you think	
Emotional	Sharing what you feel	
Transparent	Sharing who you are	

4. In what ways has your spouse's love and understanding helped you be more transparent? Think of some specific instances.

5. Describe a recent situation in which criticism or advice from your spouse stifled your transparency.

6. As you become more transparent in your relationship, what result or benefit would you expect in your marriage?

Interact as a Couple [30 minutes]
1. Discuss your answers with each other from the previous section. Remember to talk together in a loving manner.

2. Talk together about your mutual need for understanding in the areas where transparency may be stifled. Confess to each other where there has been a wrong response.

3. What are some specific steps you need to take as a couple to encourage transparency in your marriage?

4. Pray together for sensitivity and loving understanding as you communicate with each other.

Remember to take your calendar to the next session so you can Make a Date.

Listening

Conflict resolution requires a commitment to listen.

W A R M • U P   15   M I N U T E S

Back-to-Back

To start, write a list of eight things (in the left column) you would like your spouse to pick up for you at the store. Forget the diet; this is your wish list. Be specific. For example, instead of writing "milk," you might write "a half gallon of 2 percent milk."

1.	1.
2.	2.
3.	3.
4.	4.
5.	5.
6.	6.
7.	7.
8.	8.

Then, stand back-to-back with your spouse, and read aloud the list that you wrote. (Read your list only once.)

After each of you has shared your list, sit down and, with no help from your spouse, write down the eight things you're supposed to get from the store (you can write these next to your list on the previous page). After everyone finishes their lists, tell how you did. Did anyone get eight out of eight?

Now, write a new list of eight grocery items (these items should be different from the items on your first list). Get with your spouse again, but this time stand facing each other and go through your lists. You can ask questions or have your spouse repeat an item, if necessary. Then, on your own, write the things from the new list that you are supposed to get at the store.

1.   1.

2.   2.

3.   3.

4.   4.

5.   5.

6.   6.

7.   7.

8.   8.

After everyone has finished, discuss the following:
- In comparison to the first time that you tried to remember what was on your spouse's list, how did you do the second time around?

- What made the difference?

- What is the difference between "hearing" and "listening"?

Project Report
Tell of one thing you learned from the last session's HomeBuilders Project.

BLUEPRINTS   6 0   M I N U T E S

During this session, we will talk about listening. If we don't really listen to one another, we can't achieve understanding. And without understanding, it's impossible to resolve conflict. So becoming a good listener is a key step toward resolving conflict and opening the lines of communication.

The Consequences of Poor Listening

If you have a large group, break into smaller groups of about six people. In your group, read aloud the case study, using one reader for each of the three parts (Narrator, Linda, and Brian). After you read the case study, answer questions 1 through 4. After you answer, have a spokesperson report your subgroup's answers to the whole group.

Case Study: *Poor Listening Habits Fuel Conflict*

Narrator: It has been a long, trying Monday for both Brian and his wife, Linda. Fall is Brian's favorite time of year because of his love for professional football, and Monday night is his favorite night of the week. Linda enjoys an occasional game as well and has joined him in the family room. The end of the day and the smell of hot popcorn promise a pleasant evening at home together—or do they?

Linda: I wonder why our new neighbors always leave their garage door open. Wouldn't you think they would be afraid of someone stealing their things?

Brian: I don't know.

Linda: I think we need to have them over sometime. I wonder if they know anyone around here. Maybe next weekend we could invite them and some of our friends over for a barbecue.

Brian: Uh huh.

Linda: I can tell you are really concerned about these people, Brian.

Brian: Hmmmm.

Linda: Your mom called yesterday, honey. She says that all your dad wants for his birthday this year is another TV set—for the bathroom. Can you imagine, a TV set in the bathroom?

Brian: What kind does he want?

Linda: Are you just like your dad? If you had a TV in the bathroom you'd never come out—and you're in there too long as it is.

Brian: Would you mind getting some salt for the popcorn?

Linda: *(A little heated)* You get your own salt!

Brian: Now wait a minute! You know I don't want to miss any of this game. Now get the salt!

Linda: *(Sarcastically)* I think it would be all right for you to miss just a little of the game. You certainly have missed a lot of this conversation.

Brian: *(With strong emotion)* Look, I'm not in this room to be talking. Do I have to take this TV set into the bathroom to watch this game? Maybe I will go in there—at least I won't be interrupted!

Linda: *(Sarcastically)* Fine! Shall I slip the salt under the door, or do you want to come out during a commercial?

1. What poor listening habits are Brian and Linda exhibiting?

2. How do poor listening habits create conflict?

3. Put yourself in Brian and Linda's place:

- If you were Brian, how could you better listen to your wife and still enjoy the game?

- If you were Linda, what could you have done to get your husband to listen better?

4. Read Proverbs 15:1. What guidance does this verse provide for Brian and Linda? for you?

Answer question 5 with your spouse. After answering, you might want to share an appropriate insight or discovery with the group.

5. Think of a recent time when poor listening affected your relationship. What happened?

Listening Helps Defuse Conflict

6. Read James 1:19. What do you think would happen in a marriage relationship if husband and wife consistently applied these words?

If you have a large group, form smaller groups of about six people to answer the remaining Blueprints questions. Unless otherwise noted, answer the questions in your subgroup. After finishing each section, take time for subgroups to share their answers with the whole group.

7. How can taking the time to stop and listen help you avoid a conflict? Talk of a recent time when you experienced this.

8. How can you tell when your spouse really listens to you? In what ways does it strengthen your relationship?

HomeBuilders Principle:
Becoming a better listener will help you avoid many conflicts and will help you resolve other conflicts before they become too intense.

Becoming a Good Listener

9. Part of becoming a good listener involves maintaining a teachable heart. Read the following passages:

- Proverbs 1:5
- Luke 11:28

How can listening to God help you become a better listener with your spouse?

10. Another key element of becoming a good listener is giving your spouse your focused attention. This involves several elements:

- Picking the proper time and place.
- Making sure that no distractions exist.
- Maintaining eye contact.
- Allowing enough time to work through the conflict.

What have you found to be good times and places for talking about important issues and working through conflicts with your spouse? What have you found to be inappropriate places and times for this type of discussion?

11. Good listening requires more than focusing on what the person is saying. Your goal should be to truly understand what your spouse thinks, wants, and feels. What important things have you learned to do to help ensure that you understand what your spouse is saying?

12. Turn to your spouse and talk of a time God gave you greater understanding about a conflict with each other because one of you took the time to listen to the other. If appropriate, and you and your spouse are comfortable doing so, share this experience with the group.

> *"Each one speaks primarily in order to set forth his own ideas. Exceedingly few exchanges of viewpoints manifest a real desire to understand the other person."*

Dr. Paul Tournier

W R A P • U P   15   M I N U T E S

In two groups, look again at the dialogue between Brian and Linda that was presented earlier in this session. In your group, rewrite their exchange based on the components of good listening that you have been discussing. Then each group should present its version of the "new" Brian and Linda. After both groups have made presentations, answer these questions:

- What changed in how Brian and Linda communicated in the new scenarios?

- How easy is it for you to do the things you know you should do when you communicate with and listen to your spouse? Explain.

Make a Date

Make a date with your spouse to meet before the next session to complete the HomeBuilders Project. Your leader will ask at the next session for you to share one thing from this experience.

DATE

TIME

LOCATION

HOMEBUILDERS PROJECT · · · · · · · 6 0   M I N U T E S

As a Couple [10 minutes]
Start your date by taking some time to *listen* to each other. You may want to get away to a quiet place or take a short walk. Taking turns, let one spouse talk without interruption for up to 5 minutes, and then

switch. After hearing what the other person says, summarize what you understood him or her to be saying.

Individually [20 minutes]
Take some time to evaluate yourself as a listener. For questions 1 through 7, circle the response that is most true of you.

1. As your spouse talks to you, do you find it difficult to keep your mind from wandering to other things?

Yes   No   Sometimes

2. When your spouse talks, do you go beyond the facts being discussed and try to sense how he or she feels about the matter?

Yes   No   Sometimes

3. Do certain things or phrases your spouse says prejudice you so that you cannot objectively listen to what is being said?

Yes   No   Sometimes

4. When you are puzzled or annoyed by what your spouse says, do you try to get the questions straightened out as soon as possible?

Yes   No   Sometimes

5. If you believe it would take too much time and effort to understand something, do you go out of your way to avoid hearing about it?

Yes   No   Sometimes

6. When your spouse talks to you, do you try to make him or her think you are paying attention when you are not?

Yes   No   Sometimes

7. When you listen to your spouse, are you easily distracted by outside sights and sounds (such as the TV set, someone walking by, or music)?

Yes   No   Sometimes

These questions reprinted by permission from H. Norman Wright, *Communication: Key to Your Marriage* (Ventura, CA: Regal Books, 1974), 56-57.

8. What are some practical steps you can take to become a better listener?

Interact as a Couple [30 minutes]
1. Take a few minutes to discuss with each other how you evaluated yourself as a listener.

2. Talk together about what you believe your strengths and weaknesses in listening are.

3. Select an area of current conflict between you (perhaps an issue related to children, finances, a purchase, in-laws, schedules, or an upcoming social event). Each of you can take up to 5 minutes to give your point of view on the issue while the other person listens without making a comment.

After you hear from each other, explain to each other what you heard by using one or more of the following phrases:

- "What I understand you to say is..."
- "Do I understand you to mean..."
- "You may not have meant this, but what I heard you say is..."

Allow the other person to clear up any misunderstood communication. Don't necessarily seek to resolve the conflict, but simply allow for each other to speak to a listening ear.

To conclude this exercise, answer this question:

- How has this exercise in listening been helpful to you?

4. Close your time in prayer, and ask God to help you as you work to become better listeners.

Remember to take your calendar to the next session so you can Make a Date.

Confronting

Loving confrontation can help a relationship
by offering a way to practice real love.

W A R M • U P   15   M I N U T E S

What Would You Do?

As couples, pick two of the following scenarios, and
discuss with your spouse what you would most likely
do in each situation.

- You are at the store and notice someone shoplifting.

- You observe a coworker repeatedly take home of-
fice supplies.

- Your in-laws keep dropping by unexpectedly.

- You find out at a parent-teacher conference that
your child has not been turning in homework
assignments.

- Your spouse has promised to be home at a certain
time, but arrives 30 minutes late.

After discussing with your spouse the scenarios you picked, tell the group about your responses.

After everyone has had a chance to share, answer this question:

- How is confrontation in marriage different from confrontation with a stranger, family, or at work?

Project Report

Tell of one thing you learned from the last session's HomeBuilders Project.

BLUEPRINTS   60 MINUTES

Conflict can draw two people together by producing greater understanding, or it can drive a wedge of resentment and fear between them. Most of us do not deal well with conflict because we do not know how to effectively face it.

Dealing With Conflict

People typically face conflict using one of the following patterns:

Fight to Win: The "I-win-you-lose-because-I'm-right-you're-wrong" position. This pattern usually reflects domination; the relationship is valued less than triumph.

Withdraw: The "I'm-uncomfortable-so-I'll-pull-away" position. In this pattern the relationship takes on less value than avoiding the discomfort of conflict.

Yield: The "rather-than-start-another-argument-whatever-you-wish-is-fine" position. It is far better to be nice, to go along with the other person's demands, than to risk a confrontation. A safe feeling is more important than confronting the other person.

Loving Confrontation: The "I-care-enough-about-our-relationship-to-deal-with-this-issue-as-it-really-is" position. This approach offers the greatest possibility of satisfactory resolution with the least amount of threat and stress. You value the relationship more than winning or losing, escaping, or feeling comfortable.

If you have a large group, form smaller groups of about six people to answer the Blueprints questions. Unless otherwise noted, answer the questions in your subgroup. After finishing each section, take time for subgroups to relate their answers with the whole group.

1. What is your usual pattern of handling conflict in these environments:

• at work?

• with friends?

• with your family?

• with your spouse?

2. How has your pattern of dealing with conflict changed over time? What factors would you say most influence your approach to handling conflict?

3. How do you think your pattern affects your spouse?

Examples of Conflict From the Bible

The Bible is filled with stories of real people—people in conflict. Look at the following Bible passages, and determine which style of dealing with conflict they describe.

4. In Genesis 3, after Adam and Eve had eaten the forbidden fruit, God was in the garden looking for them.

- According to Genesis 3:8-10, how did Adam and Eve respond to this conflict with God? Which of the patterns did Adam employ?

- In what ways do couples often respond to each other like Adam and Eve did to God?

5. Read Mark 15:9-15. In this situation Pilate had a decision to make.

- What did Pilate do to resolve the conflict he had with the crowd?

• What problems does this approach create in a marriage?

6. Read 1 Samuel 20:33. King Saul has discovered that his son, Jonathan, was befriending young David, the object of the king's intense jealousy.
• What was Saul's apparent pattern for handling conflict?

• What is the danger in marriage with this kind of response?

7. Read Luke 10:38-42.
• How did Jesus deal with conflict in this situation?

• What does it take to react to conflict like Jesus did here?

Steps Toward Loving Confrontation

The words "loving" and "confrontation" don't appear to be complementary. One word is friendly, and the other word makes you want to fight back. However, the combination of these two words—"loving confrontation"—provides an important approach to resolving conflict. Loving confrontation is the balanced use of truth and love.

Step One: *Look inward.*
Read Galatians 6:1-2 and Matthew 7:3-5.

8. Why is looking inward before confrontation important? Why is your attitude important in confrontation?

Step Two: *Pick the right time and place.*
Read Proverbs 25:11.

Answer questions 9 and 10 with your spouse. After you answer, you may want to share an appropriate insight or discovery with the group.

9. Proverbs 25:11 talks about "a word spoken in right circumstances" (New American Standard Bible). What might be some "right circumstances" for loving confrontation in your marriage?

10. What are typically appropriate and inappropriate times or settings for your spouse to bring up a difficult but necessary issue with you?

Step Three: *Speak the truth in love.*
Read Ephesians 4:15-16 and 1 Corinthians 13:4-5.

11. What do you think it means to speak "the truth in love"? What happens when truth is spoken without love, or when there is love without truth?

12. Which is easier for you—to speak the truth without love, or to love without speaking the truth? Why?

HomeBuilders Principle:
*For confrontation to benefit a relationship,
truth must be shared with love.*

In a confrontation, one of the most effective techniques is to turn "you" messages into "I" messages. For example, instead of declaring, "You don't understand me," say, "I feel misunderstood." This helps your spouse focus on the problem rather than on personal failure.

"I" messages are usually clear and honest. "I" messages don't place blame. "You" messages are most often attacks and criticisms. They seek to fix blame on the other person.

Following is a list of "you" messages. As a group, take a minute to brainstorm a few more "you" messages to add to the list. Then with your spouse, turn the "you" messages into "I" messages.

"You" Messages	"I" Messages
You don't understand me!	I feel misunderstood!
You don't budget our money!	I'm concerned about our finances. Can you help me?
You are gone too much!	
You are always late!	
You always blame everything on me!	

continued on page 62

continued from page 61

"You" Messages	**"I" Messages**
You make me angry!	
You never tell me you love me!	

Tell the group about a couple of "I" messages that you and your spouse came up with. After everyone has shared, take a moment of silence to think about a particular "you" message that you find yourself using with your spouse. Pray silently by yourself, asking God to help you better communicate with your spouse.

Make a Date

Make a date with your spouse to meet before the next session to complete the HomeBuilders Project. At the next session, your leader will ask you to share one thing from this experience.

DATE

TIME

LOCATION

As a Couple [10 minutes]

Discuss with your spouse what you most likely would do in each of the following situations. Remember, be kind—and have fun with this!

- You receive a notice that your auto insurance rates are going up because of a recent speeding ticket. Your spouse had neglected to tell you about getting a ticket.

- You are lost, but your spouse refuses to stop and ask for directions.

- You notice that your spouse is using your favorite T-shirt to clean the bathroom.

- Your spouse was going to stop at the cleaners to pick up the outfit you plan to wear to an important meeting the next day. Your spouse arrives home having forgotten to go by the cleaners, and now the cleaners is closed.

Now, go back through as many of the scenarios as you have time to, and in place of what your likely response would be, talk about what "loving confrontation" might look like in each situation.

Individually [20 minutes]

1. What is one way this session challenged you in the way you approach confrontation?

2. Think of a recent misunderstanding between you and your spouse. Think about how you responded. Which pattern most reflects how you responded? (Circle your answer.)
- Fight to Win
- Withdraw
- Yield
- Loving Confrontation

Now, think about how your spouse reacted. Put a check next to the pattern you believe reflects how your spouse reacted.

Answer these questions:
- What could you do differently next time?

- What would you prefer your spouse to do differently next time?

3. Loving confrontation turns accusatory when you approach it without the proper focus. Check the areas that you tend to have out of focus when you confront your spouse:

___ Raising many issues at once instead of just one issue at a time.

___ Focusing on the person rather than the problem.

___ Bringing up the past instead of sticking to the present.

___ Using generalizations rather than specifics.

___ Using "you" statements rather than "I" statements.

___ Judging motives rather than observing facts.

___ Judging actions rather than expressing feelings.

___ Concentrating on who is winning or losing rather than striving for mutual understanding.

4. What can you do to keep confrontation with your spouse in focus?

Interact as a Couple [30 minutes]
1. Go through your answers to the questions from the individual time.

2. Reach a consensus on some ground rules you would like to use in dealing with confrontation in your marriage.

3. Ask the Lord for his wisdom and help in dealing with conflict and confrontation in your marriage.

Remember to take your calendar to the next session so you can Make a Date.

Forgiving

For peace to replace conflict, husband and wife must take responsibility to forgive each other.

W A R M • U P   15   M I N U T E S

"To Err Is Human, to Forgive Divine"

Choose one or two of the following questions to answer and relate to the group:

- When you were a child, who taught you the most about what forgiveness is? How did this person teach you?

- From your childhood, when was a time you especially remember having to say, "I'm sorry"?

- Other than Christ, who do you look to as an example of a forgiving person? Why?

Project Report

Tell of one thing you learned from the last session's HomeBuilders Project.

The Importance of Forgiveness

If you have a large group, form smaller groups of about six people to answer the Blueprints questions. Unless otherwise noted, answer the questions in your subgroup. After finishing each section, take time for subgroups to relate their answers with the whole group.

1. What would you say it means to forgive another person?

2. Think about a time you received forgiveness from another person for something you did. How did you feel before and after you received forgiveness?

3. The most profound example of forgiveness is God's forgiveness of us. Each couple should take one of the following verses. With your spouse, read your verse and discuss what it says about God's forgiveness. Then talk about your verse and insights with the group.

- John 3:16
- Romans 8:1
- 2 Corinthians 5:19
- Ephesians 1:7
- Colossians 2:13
- Hebrews 10:14

4. Why is the kind of forgiveness described in the previous verses so essential in a marriage relationship?

5. Read Matthew 6:14-15 and Matthew 18:21-22. What is profound about what Jesus says about forgiveness?

HomeBuilders Principle:
To maintain a healthy marriage relationship, you must forgive your spouse as God has forgiven you.

Asking for Forgiveness

6. Read Luke 15:11-24. What steps did the prodigal son take to seek forgiveness from his father?

7. Why is each of these steps important in the process of receiving forgiveness?

Answer questions 8 and 9 with your spouse. After answering, you may want to share an appropriate insight or discovery with the group.

8. Generally speaking, do you find it easier to ask your spouse for forgiveness or to extend forgiveness to you spouse? Explain.

9. Why is it often so difficult to request forgiveness or grant forgiveness in marriage?

HomeBuilders Principle:
Forgiving your spouse sets you free to experience love and oneness in your marriage.

Granting Forgiveness

Step One: *Give up the right of punishment.*
Read Ephesians 4:17, 22-24, 31-32.

10. What does this passage tell us to do with our feelings?

Step Two: *Yield yourself to the control of the Holy Spirit.*
Read Romans 8:5-6; 12-14.

11. How does living under the control of the Holy Spirit empower you to forgive your spouse?

Step Three: Choose not to dwell on the past.
Read Isaiah 43:18-19.

12. How can this passage be applied to forgiveness in marriage?

HomeBuilder's Principle:
The power to forgive comes from God's Spirit as you give him control of your life.

W R A P • U P   15 M I N U T E S

Read the case study and discuss the questions that follow.

Marriage Trouble

Case Study

Charlie and Beth have come to you for help. They are Christians, married for twelve years. You are relieved to hear that they have been faithful to each other, but you wonder how their resentment toward each other has grown. They express the core of their frustrations:

Beth: Charlie makes me feel so unlovable. He always has to be right. The things he has said to me when he's angry, the way he treats me around the kids, his arrogant ways in front of my in-laws—I just can't let him get by with this. Why should I forgive him? He made his bed, let him lie in it!

Charlie: If I've hurt her, then she deserves it. I work hard all day to provide for her and the children and all I hear is griping. I can never do enough, never say things just right, never be kind enough to her folks. She's done more than her share to make me miserable. I'm only balancing the scales!

- What do you think might have contributed to this couple's coldness toward each other? (This is a good time to think back over previous sessions to draw from them possible causes of conflict between Charlie and Beth.)

- If Charlie and Beth don't change, what do you see happening in their relationship?

- How would you counsel them?

- In addition to forgiving each other, what else do Charlie and Beth need to do?

Make a Date

Make a date with your spouse to meet before the next session to complete the HomeBuilders Project. Your leader will ask at the next session for you to share one thing from this experience.

DATE

TIME

LOCATION

As a Couple [10 minutes]

Before getting into the serious topic of asking for and granting forgiveness, take a few minutes to focus on the lighter side of this issue—the fun of making up! Discuss these questions together:

- What is something you recall your spouse doing that was his or her attempt to "make up"?

- What are some creative ideas for ways that you can make up with your spouse?

Individually [20 minutes]

1. Look back over this session. What was the key insight you gained?

2. Read Ephesians 4:32. How can you apply "forgiving...just as in Christ God forgave you" when...

- you think about things your spouse has done to you in the past?

- you want to remind your spouse of a way he or she has hurt you in the past?

3. Complete the following statements:

- My greatest difficulty in offering my spouse forgiveness is...

- The one thing that would make it easier for me to ask for my spouse's forgiveness is ...

4. What is an instance in which you received forgiveness from your spouse and healing occurred in your relationship as a result?

5. Have you accepted God's offer of forgiveness to you through his son, Jesus? If you're not sure, read the article "Our Problems, God's Answers" starting on page 93.

6. What, if anything, is something for which you need to ask your spouse's forgiveness?

7. Pray, thanking God for his forgiveness and asking him to help you live according to the Spirit. Pray that you would be gracious toward your spouse in both extending and receiving forgiveness.

Interact as a Couple [30 minutes]

1. Discuss your answers to questions 1 through 5 in the previous section.

2. Discuss what you can do to make it easier for each other to admit wrong and seek forgiveness.

3. Now it's time to practice what you've been learning. Discuss your response to question 6 in the previous section.

4. Pray together. Thank God for his unending grace and the Holy Spirit who enables you to forgive each other "as in Christ God forgave you."

Remember to take your calendar to the next session so you can Make a Date.

A Blessing for an Insult

People naturally tend to respond to hurts with anger. God promises to help us exchange these natural reactions for supernatural responses.

W A R M • U P   15   M I N U T E S

Insults and Blessings

Think about the past week. What are some insults you heard others speak? Share one example with the group.

Now think of an uplifting, positive word—a word of blessing. Using this word, write a sentence that affirms your spouse, then share with your mate what you wrote.

After everyone has shared their sentences, discuss these questions as a group:

- Which was easier to think of—an insult or a blessing? Why?
- How did it feel to receive a word of blessing from your spouse?

Project Report

Tell the group about one thing you learned from the last session's HomeBuilders Project.

BLUEPRINTS   60 MINUTES

Since hurt and disappointment are inevitable in marriage, we need to decide how we want to respond. We have a choice—we can return an insult with another insult, or we can give a blessing instead.

Insult for Insult

If you have a large group, form smaller groups of about six people to answer the Blueprints questions. Unless otherwise noted, answer the questions in your subgroup. After finishing each section, take time for subgroups to relate their answers with the whole group.

1. Read 1 Peter 3:8-9. What does "repay evil with evil or insult with insult" mean? What does it look like in a marriage relationship?

2. Read 1 Peter 2:23. Descirbe how Christ responded to insult? To what extent do you think we are to follow Christ's example? Explain.

3. When have you seen an insult-for-insult type of response in your marriage?

Answer questions 3 and 4 with your spouse. After answering, you may want to share an appropriate insight or discovery with the group.

4. What situations or circumstances tend to provoke this type of response for you?

Blessing for Insult

5. Read 1 Peter 3:8-9 again. What does it mean to repay or give a blessing? What example comes to mind?

6. Read Luke 6:27-28 and Romans 12:14-21. What additional insights do you gain from these verses about giving a blessing from these challenging passages?

7. Why is giving a blessing after an insult often so difficult?

8. What are some practical ways you can give a blessing?

HomeBuilders Principle:
Returning a blessing for an insult helps defeat the cycle of selfishness that can corrode a marriage relationship.

Relationship Comparison

Insult-for-Insult Relationship	Blessing-for-Blessing Relationship
1. Human perspective	1. Divine perspective
2. Based on selfishness and circumstances	2. Based on God's Word, the unseen
3. Results: punishment, anger, and barriers	3. Results: purposeful action, transparency
4. Reactive: emotionally centered; following natural instincts	4. Responsive: God-centered, supernatural response
5. Attitude: tear down; depreciate; provoke the other person more	5. Attitude: build up; appreciate; provoke confession, godliness, and blessing

A Blessing Relationship

Read 1 Peter 3:10-11. This passage outlines three simple steps for establishing a blessing relationship:

Step One: *Keep your tongue from evil.*

9. Why is control of one's tongue so important to the establishment of a blessing relationship?

Step Two: *"Turn from evil and do good."*

10. How do you "turn from evil"? What effect does this response have on a conflict?

Step Three: *"Seek peace and pursue it."*

11. The words "seek" and "pursue" are actions. What types of things should you seek and pursue in marriage to bring about peace and blessing?

12. Read Philippians 2:3-8. Giving a blessing adopting an attitude of regarding another person as more important than you are. What are some examples of how you could give a blessing by doing what your spouse wants instead of what you want?

Take a few minutes to review the following questions.
Write responses to the questions you can answer. Then,
as a group, reflect on your experience by relating
your answers.

- What has this group meant to you during the
  course of this study? Be specific.

- What is one valuable thing you learned or discovered?

- How have you, or your marriage, been changed or
  challenged?

- What would you like to see happen next for this
  group?

Make a Date

Make a date with your spouse to meet this week to complete this study's last HomeBuilders Project.

DATE

TIME

LOCATION

HOMEBUILDERS PROJECT   6 0   M I N U T E S

As a Couple [10 minutes]
Congratulations—you've made it to the last project for this study! To start this date, reflect on how this study has affected your marriage and answer these questions:

- Thinking back to the first meeting of this study, what expectations did you have of this course? How did your experience compare to your expectations?

- What is something from this study that has helped your marriage?

- What is something new you learned about your spouse?

• What has been the best part of this study for you?

Individually [20 minutes]

1. How have the principles you've learned during this study helped you begin to resolve conflict in your marriage?

2. What are some principles that you need to practice or emphasize more?

3. People typically react to an insult by either withdrawing or attacking. How would you rate your tendencies to withdraw or attack in response to conflict? (Circle the appropriate number on the scale.)

Withdraw

1	2	3	4	5	6	7	8	9	10
low									high

Attack

1	2	3	4	5	6	7	8	9	10
low									high

4. How would you rate your spouse's tendencies?

Withdraw

1	2	3	4	5	6	7	8	9	10
low									high

Attack

1	2	3	4	5	6	7	8	9	10
low									high

5. Use the following chart to become a better student of yourself and your reactions.

- Consider the situations in which you tend to react against your spouse. List them in the first column of the chart.

- In the second column, list your typical responses to each situation.

- Rank the magnitude of the problems caused by each situation as high (H), medium (M), or low (L), and list your ranking in the third column.

- In the fourth column, list how you think you should respond to each situation.

Situation	Usual Response	Magnitude of Problem	Better Response

6. How can you "seek peace and pursue it" on a more consistent basis in your marriage relationship?

Interact as a Couple [30 minutes]
1. Discuss together your answers from the previous section with each other.

2. Read 1 Peter 2:23. Talk about what "entrusting" yourself "to him who judges justly" means. Why is this important when you're working through conflict? How might you know when your spouse is doing this?

3. Evaluate what you might do together to continue building your marriage, as well as building up one another and others. One thing you may consider is continuing the practice of setting aside time as you have for these projects. You may also want to look at several ideas on page 91 in "Where Do You Go From Here?"

4. Pray together, asking the Lord to give you wisdom as you seek to practice returning a blessing for an insult in your relationships.

Please visit our Web site at www.familylife.com/homebuilders
to give us your feedback on this study and to get information
on other FamilyLife resources and conferences.

Where Do You Go From Here?

It is our prayer that you have benefited greatly from this study in the HomeBuilders Couples Series. We hope that your marriage will continue to grow as you both submit your lives to Jesus Christ and build according to his blueprints.

We also hope that you will begin reaching out to strengthen other marriages in your community and local church. Your church needs couples like you who are committed to building Christian marriages. A favorite World War II story illustrates this point very clearly.

The year was 1940. The French Army had just collapsed under Hitler's onslaught. The Dutch had folded, overwhelmed by the Nazi regime. The Belgians had surrendered. And the British Army was trapped on the coast of France in the channel port of Dunkirk.

Two hundred and twenty thousand of Britain's finest young men seemed doomed to die, turning the English Channel red with their blood. The Fuehrer's troops, only miles away in the hills of France, didn't realize how close to victory they actually were.

Any rescue seemed feeble and futile in the time remaining. A "thin" British Navy—"the professionals"—told King George VI that at best they could save 17,000 troops. The House of Commons was warned to prepare for "hard and heavy tidings."

Politicians were paralyzed. The king was powerless. And the Allies could only watch as spectators from a distance. Then as the doom of the British Army seemed imminent, a strange fleet appeared on the horizon of the English Channel—the wildest assortment of boats perhaps ever assembled in history.

Trawlers, tugs, scows, fishing sloops, lifeboats, pleasure craft, smacks and coasters, sailboats, even the London fire-brigade flotilla. *Each ship was manned by civilian volunteers—English fathers sailing to rescue Britain's exhausted, bleeding sons.*

William Manchester writes in his epic novel, *The Last Lion*, that even today what happened in 1940 in less than twenty-four hours seems like a miracle—not only were all of the British soldiers rescued, but 118,000 other Allied troops as well.

Today the Christian home is much like those troops at Dunkirk. Pressured, trapped, and demoralized, it needs help. Your help. The Christian community may be much like England—we stand waiting for politicians, professionals, even for our pastors to step in and save the family. But the problem is much larger than all of those combined can solve.

With the highest divorce rate of any nation on earth, we need an all-out effort by men and women "sailing" to rescue the exhausted and wounded family casualties. We need an outreach effort by common couples with faith in an uncommon God. For too long, married couples within the church have abdicated the privilege and responsibility of influencing others to those in full-time vocational ministry.

Possibly this study has indeed been used to "light the torch" of your spiritual lives. Perhaps it was already burning, and this provided more fuel. Regardless, may we challenge you to invest your lives in others?

You and other couples around the world can team together to build thousands of marriages and families. By starting a HomeBuilders group, you will not only strengthen other marriages; you will also see your marriage grow as you share these principles with others.

Will You Join Us in "Touching Lives...Changing Families"?

The following are some practical ways you can make a difference in families today:

1. Gather a group of four to eight couples, and lead them through the six sessions of this HomeBuilders study, *Resolving Conflict in Your Marriage*. (Why not consider challenging others in your church or community to form additional HomeBuilders groups?)

2. Commit to continue marriage building by doing another course in the HomeBuilders Couples Series.

3. An excellent outreach tool is the film "*JESUS,*" which is available on video. For more information, contact FamilyLife at 1-800-FL-TODAY.

4. Host a dinner party. Invite families from your neighborhood to your home, and as a couple share your faith in Christ.

5. Reach out and share the love of Christ with neighborhood children.

6. If you have attended the FamilyLife Marriage Conference, why not offer to assist your pastor in counseling couples engaged to be married, using the material you received?

For more information about any of the above ministry opportunities, contact your local church, or write:

> **FamilyLife**
> P.O. Box 8220
> Little Rock, AR 72221-8220
> 1-800-FL-TODAY
> **www.familylife.com**

Our Problems, God's Answers

●

Every couple eventually has to deal with problems in marriage. Communication problems. Money problems. Difficulties with sexual intimacy. These issues are important to cultivating a strong, loving relationship with your spouse. The HomeBuilders Couples Series is designed to help you strengthen your marriage in many of these critical areas.

Part One: The Big Problem

One basic problem is at the heart of every other problem in every marriage, and it's a problem we can't help you fix. No matter how hard you try, this is one problem that is too big for you to deal with on your own.

The problem is separation from God. If you want to experience marriage the way it was designed to be, you need a vital relationship with the God who created you and offers you the power to live a life of joy and purpose.

And what separates us from God is one more problem—sin. Most of us have assumed throughout our lives that the term "sin" refers to a list of bad habits that everyone agrees are wrong. We try to deal with our sin problem by working hard to become better people. We read books to learn how to control our anger, or we resolve to stop cheating on our taxes.

But in our hearts, we know our sin problem runs much deeper than a list of bad habits. All of us have rebelled against God. We have ignored him and have decided to run our own lives in a way that makes sense to us. The Bible says that the God who created us wants us to follow his plan for our lives. But because of our sin problem, we think our ideas and plans are better than his.

- *"For all have sinned and fall short of the glory of God"* (Romans 3:23).

What does it mean to "fall short of the glory of God"? It means that none of us has trusted and treasured God the way we should. We have sought to satisfy ourselves with other things and have treated those things as more valuable than God. We have gone our own way. According to the Bible, we have to pay a penalty for our sin. We cannot simply do things the way we choose and hope it will all be OK with God. Following our own plan leads to our destruction.

- *"There is a way that seems right to a man, but in the end it leads to death"* (Proverbs 14:12).

- *"For the wages of sin is death"* (Romans 6:23a).

The penalty for sin is that we are forever separated from God's love. God is holy, and we are sinful. No matter how hard we try, we cannot come up with some plan, like living a good life or even trying to do what the Bible says, and hope that we can avoid the penalty.

God's Solution to Sin

Thankfully God has a way to solve our dilemma. He became a man through the person of Jesus Christ. He lived a holy life, in perfect obedience to God's plan. He also willingly died on a cross to pay our penalty for sin. Then he proved that he is more powerful than sin or death by rising from the dead. He alone has the power to overrule the penalty for our sin.

- *"Jesus answered, 'I am the way and the truth and the life. No one comes to the Father except through me'"* (John 14:6).

- *"But God demonstrates his own love for us in this: While we were still sinners, Christ died for us"* (Romans 5:8).

- *"Christ died for our sins…he was buried…he was raised on the third day according to the Scriptures…he appeared to Peter, and then to the Twelve. After that, he appeared to more than five hundred"* (1 Corinthians 15:3-6).

- *"For the wages of sin is death, but the gift of God is eternal life in Christ Jesus our Lord"* (Romans 6:23).

The death of Jesus has fixed our sin problem. He has bridged the gap between God and us. He is calling all of us to come to him and to give up our own flawed plan for how to run our lives. He wants us to trust God and his plan.

Accepting God's Solution

If you agree that you are separated from God, he is calling you to confess your sins. All of us have made messes of our lives because we have stubbornly preferred our ideas and plans over his. As a result, we deserve to be cut off from God's love and his care for us. But God has promised that if we will agree that we have rebelled against his plan for us and have messed up our lives, he will forgive us and will fix our sin problem.

- *"Yet to all who received him, to those who believed in his name, he gave the right to become children of God"* (John 1:12).

- *"For it is by grace you have been saved, through faith—and this not from yourselves, it is the gift of*

God—not by works, so that no one can boast" (Ephesians 2:8-9).

When the Bible talks about receiving Christ, it means we acknowledge that we are sinners and that we can't fix the problem ourselves. It means we turn away from our sin. And it means we trust Christ to forgive our sins and to make us the kind of people he wants us to be. It's not enough to just intellectually believe that Christ is the Son of God. We must trust in him and his plan for our lives by faith, as an act of the will.

Are things right between you and God, with him and his plan at the center of your life? Or is life spinning out of control as you seek to make your way on your own?

You can decide today to make a change. You can turn to Christ and allow him to transform your life. All you need to do is to talk to him and tell him what is stirring in your mind and in your heart. If you've never done this before, considering taking the steps listed here:

- Do you agree that you need God? Tell God.

- Have you made a mess of your life by following your own plan? Tell God.

- Do you want God to forgive you? Tell God.

- Do you believe that Jesus' death on the cross and his resurrection from the dead gave him the power to fix your sin problem and to grant you the gift of eternal life? Tell God.

- Are you ready to acknowledge that God's plan for your life is better than any plan you could come up with? Tell God.

- Do you agree that God has the right to be the Lord and master of your life? Tell God.

> *"Seek the Lord while he may be found;*
> *call on him while he is near"*
> (Isaiah 55:6).

Following is a suggested prayer:

> *Lord Jesus, I need you. Thank you for dying on the*
> *cross for my sins. I receive you as my Savior and Lord.*
> *Thank you for forgiving my sins and giving me eternal*
> *life. Make me the kind of person you want me to be.*

Does this prayer express the desire of your heart? If it does, pray it right now, and Christ will come into your life, as he promised.

Part Two: Living the Christian Life

For a person who is a follower of Christ—a Christian—the penalty for sin is paid in full. But the effect of sin continues throughout our lives.

- *"If we claim to be without sin, we deceive ourselves and the truth is not in us"* (1 John 1:8).

- *"For what I do is not the good I want to do; no, the evil I do not want to do—this I keep on doing"* (Romans 7:19).

The effects of sin carry over into our marriages as well. Even Christians struggle to maintain solid, God-honoring marriages. Most couples eventually realize that they can't do it on their own. But with God's help, they can succeed. The Holy Spirit can have a huge impact in the marriages of Christians who live constantly, moment by moment, under his gracious direction.

Self-Centered Christians

Many Christians struggle to live the Christian life in their own strength because they are not allowing God to control their lives. Their interests are self-directed, often resulting in failure and frustration.

- *"Brothers, I could not address you as spiritual but as worldly—mere infants in Christ. I gave you milk, not solid food, for you were not yet ready for it. Indeed, you are still not ready. You are still worldly. For since there is jealousy and quarreling among you, are you not worldly? Are you not acting like mere men?"* (1 Corinthians 3:1-3).

The self-centered Christian cannot experience the abundant and fruitful Christian life. Such people trust in their own efforts to live the Christian life: They are either uninformed about—or have forgotten—God's love, forgiveness, and power. This kind of Christian:

- has an up-and-down spiritual experience.

- cannot understand himself—he wants to do what is right, but cannot.

- fails to draw upon the power of the Holy Spirit to live the Christian life.

Some or all of the following traits may characterize the Christian who does not fully trust God:

disobedience	plagued by impure thoughts
lack of love for God and others	jealous
	worrisome
inconsistent prayer life	easily discouraged, frustrated
lack of desire for Bible study	critical
legalistic attitude	lack of purpose

Note: The individual who professes to be a Christian but who continues to practice sin should realize that he may not be a Christian at all, according to 1 John 2:3, 3:6, 9; Ephesians 5:5.

Spirit-Centered Christians

When a Christian puts Christ on the throne of his life, he yields to God's control. This Christian's interests are directed by the Holy Spirit, resulting in harmony with God's plan.

- *"But the fruit of the Spirit is love, joy, peace, patience, kindness, goodness, faithfulness, gentleness and self-control. Against such things there is no law"* (Galatians 5:22-23).

Jesus said,

- *"I have come that they may have life, and have it to the full"* (John 10:10b).

- *"I am the vine; you are the branches. If a man remains in me and I in him, he will bear much fruit; apart from me you can do nothing"* (John 15:5).

- *"But you will receive power when the Holy Spirit comes on you; and you will be my witnesses in Jerusalem, and in all Judea and Samaria, and to the ends of the earth"* (Acts 1:8).

The following traits result naturally from the Holy Spirit's work in our lives:

Christ centered	love
Holy Spirit empowered	joy
motivated to tell others about Jesus	peace
	patience
dedicated to prayer	kindness
student of God's Word	goodness
trusts God	faithfulness
obeys God	gentleness
	self-control

The degree to which these traits appear in a Christian's life and marriage depends upon the extent to which the Christian trusts the Lord with every detail of life, and upon that person's maturity in Christ. One who is only beginning to understand the ministry of the Holy Spirit should not be discouraged if he is not as fruitful as mature Christians who have known and experienced this truth for a longer period of time.

Giving God Control

Jesus promises his followers an abundant and fruitful life as they allow themselves to be directed and empowered by the Holy Spirit. As we give God control of our lives, Christ lives in and through us in the power of the Holy Spirit (John 15).

If you sincerely desire to be directed and empowered by God, you can turn your life over to the control of the Holy Spirit right now (Matthew 5:6; John 7:37-39).

First, confess your sins to God, agreeing with him that you want to turn from any past sinful patterns in your life. Thank God in faith that he has forgiven all of your sins because Christ died for you (Colossians 2:13-15; 1 John 1:9; 2:1-3; Hebrews 10:1-18).

Be sure to offer every area of your life to God (Romans 12:1-2). Consider what areas you might rather keep to yourself, and be sure you're willing to give God control in those areas.

By faith, commit yourself to living according to the Holy Spirit's guidance and power.

- *Live by the Spirit: "So I say, live by the Spirit, and you will not gratify the desires of the sinful nature. For the sinful nature desires what is contrary to the Spirit, and the Spirit what is contrary to the sinful nature. They are in conflict with each other, so that you do not do what you want"* (Galatians 5:16-17).

- *Trust in God's Promise: "This is the confidence we have in approaching God: that if we ask anything according to his will, he hears us. And if we know that he hears us—whatever we ask—we know that we have what we asked of him"* (1 John 5:14-15).

Expressing Your Faith Through Prayer

Prayer is one way of expressing your faith to God. If the prayer that follows expresses your sincere desire, consider praying the prayer or putting the thoughts into your own words:

Dear God, I need you. I acknowledge that I have been directing my own life and that, as a result, I have sinned against you. I thank you that you have forgiven my sins through Christ's death on the cross for me. I now invite Christ to take his place on the throne of my life. Take control of my life through the Holy Spirit as you promised you would if I asked in faith. I now thank you for directing my life and for empowering me through the Holy Spirit.

Walking in the Spirit

If you become aware of an area of your life (an attitude or an action) that is displeasing to God, simply confess your sin, and thank God that he has forgiven your sins on the basis of Christ's death on the cross. Accept God's love and forgiveness by faith, and continue to have fellowship with him.

If you find that you've taken back control of your life through sin—a definite act of disobedience—try this exercise, "Spiritual Breathing," as you give that control back to God.

1. Exhale. Confess your sin. Agree with God that you've sinned against him, and thank him for his forgiveness of it, according to 1 John 1:9 and Hebrews 10:1-25. Remember that confession involves repentance, a determination to change attitudes and actions.

2. Inhale. Surrender control of your life to Christ, inviting the Holy Spirit to once again take charge. Trust that he now directs and empowers you, according to the command of Galatians 5:16-17 and the promise of 1 John 5:14-15. Returning to your faith in God enables you to continue to experience God's love and forgiveness.

Revolutionizing Your Marriage

This new commitment of your life to God will enrich your marriage. Sharing with your spouse what you've committed to is a powerful step in solidifying this commitment. As you exhibit the Holy Spirit's work within you, your spouse may be drawn to make the same commitment you've made. If both of you have given control of your life to the Holy Spirit, you'll be able to help each other remain true to God, and your marriage may be revolutionized. With God in charge of your lives, life becomes an amazing adventure.

Leader's Notes

Contents

About Leading a HomeBuilders Group

What is the leader's job?

Your role is that of "facilitator"—one who encourages people to think and to discover what Scripture says, who helps group members feel comfortable, and who keeps things moving forward.

What is the best setting and time schedule for this study?

This study is designed as a small group home Bible study. However, it can be adapted for use in a Sunday school setting as well. Here are some suggestions for using this study in a small group and in a Sunday school class:

In a small group

To create a friendly and comfortable atmosphere, it is recommended that you do this study in a home setting. In many cases the couple that leads the study also serves as host to the group. Sometimes involving another couple as host is a good idea. Choose the option you believe will work best for your group, taking into account factors such as the number of couples participating and the location.

Each session is designed as a ninety-minute study, but we recommend a two-hour block of time. This will allow you to move through each part of the study at a more relaxed pace. However, be sure to keep in mind one of the cardinal rules of a small group: Good groups start *and* end on time. People's time is valuable, and your group will appreciate you being respectful of this.

In a Sunday school class

There are two important adaptations you need to make if you want to use this study in a class setting: 1) The material you cover should focus on the content from the Blueprints section of each session. Blueprints is the heart of each session and is designed to last sixty minutes. 2) Most Sunday school classes are taught in a teacher format instead of a small group format. If this study will be used in a class setting, the class should adapt to a small group dynamic. This will involve an interactive, discussion-based format and may also require a class to break into multiple smaller groups (we recommend groups of six to eight people).

What is the best size group?

We recommend from four to eight couples (including you and your spouse). If you have more people interested than you think you can accommodate, consider asking someone else to lead a second group. If you have a large group, you are encouraged at various times in the study to break into smaller subgroups. This helps you cover the material in a timely fashion and allows for optimum interaction and participation within the group.

What about refreshments?

Many groups choose to serve refreshments, which help create an environment of fellowship. If you plan on including refreshments in your study, here are a couple of suggestions: 1) For the first session (or two) you should provide the refreshments and then allow the group to be involved by having people sign up to bring them on later dates. 2) Consider starting your group with a short time of informal fellowship and refreshments (fifteen minutes), then move into the study. If couples are late, they miss only the food and don't disrupt the study. You may also want to have refreshments available at the end of your meeting to encourage fellowship; but remember, respect the group members' time by ending the study on schedule and allowing anyone who needs to leave right away the opportunity to do so gracefully.

What about child care?

Groups handle this differently depending on their needs. Here are a couple of options you may want to consider:

- Have group members be responsible for making their own arrangements.

- As a group, hire child care, and have all the kids watched in one location.

What about prayer?

An important part of a small group is prayer. However, as the leader, you need to be sensitive to the level of comfort the people in your group have toward praying in front of others. Never call on people to pray aloud if you don't know if they are comfortable doing this. There are a number of creative approaches you can take, such as modeling prayer, calling for volunteers, and letting people state their prayers in the form of finishing a sentence. A tool that is helpful in a group is a prayer list. You are encouraged to do this, but let it be someone else's ministry to the group. You should lead the prayer time, but allow another couple in the group the opportunity to create, update, and distribute prayer lists.

In closing

An excellent resource that covers leading a HomeBuilders group in greater detail is the *HomeBuilders Leader Guide* by Drew and Kit Coons. This book may be obtained at your local Christian bookstore or by contacting Group Publishing or FamilyLife.

About the
Leader's Notes

The sessions in this study can be easily led without a lot of preparation time. However, accompanying Leader's Notes have been provided to assist you in preparation. The categories within the Leader's Notes are as follows:

Objectives

The purpose of the Objectives is to help focus the issues that will be presented in each session.

Notes and Tips

This section will relate any general comments about the session. This information should be viewed as ideas, helps, and suggestions. You may want to create a checklist of things you want to be sure to do in each session.

Commentary

Included in this section are notes that relate specifically to Blueprints questions. Not all Blueprints questions in each session will have accompanying commentary notes. Questions with related commentaries are designated by numbers (for example, Blueprints question 5 in Session One would correspond to number 5 in the Commentary section of Session One Leader's Notes).

Session One:
Recognizing Conflict

Objectives

God's design for marriage leads to a meaningful and valued relationship between husband and wife. Since conflict is inevitable in marriage, we must discover how to use it in building this relationship through communication and understanding.

In this session, couples will...

• examine factors that contribute to conflict in a relationship.

• discuss the effect of conflict.

• study scriptural guidance for pursuing peace.

Notes and Tips

1. If you have not already done so, read "About the Sessions" on pages 4 and 5 as well as "About Leading a HomeBuilders Group" and "About the Leader's Notes" starting on page 104.

2. As part of the first session, review with the group some Ground Rules (see page 12 in the Introduction).

3. Be sure you have a study guide for each person. You will also need to have extra Bibles, and pens or pencils.

4. Because this is the first session, make a special point to tell the group about the importance of the HomeBuilders

Project. Encourage each couple to "Make a Date" to complete the project before the next meeting. Mention that you will ask about results during the next session's Warm-Up.

5. If the group has not been together before, have couples introduce themselves during the Warm-Up. One way to do this is to have couples briefly share how and when they met. If you choose to do this, you will probably spend more than 15 minutes for Warm-Up. If this happens, try to finish Blueprints in 45 to 60 minutes. It is a good idea to mark the questions in Blueprints that you want to be sure to cover. For any questions that you might not cover during the session, suggest to the group that they plan on looking at those questions as a part of the HomeBuilders Project.

6. A note at the start of Blueprints recommends breaking into smaller groups. The reason for this is twofold: 1) to help facilitate discussion and participation by everyone, and 2) to help you get through the material in the allotted time.

Similarly, Blueprints question 9 calls for couples to look up one of the Scripture passages in this question. This is done so multiple passages can be studied simultaneously. This saves time and gives the group an opportunity to learn from each other.

7. Because this is the first session, consider offering a closing prayer instead of asking others to pray aloud. Many people are uncomfortable praying in front of others, and unless you already know your group well, it may be wise to slowly venture into various methods of prayer. Regardless of how you decide to close, you should serve as a model.

8. With this group just getting under way, remind the group that it's not too late to invite another couple to join the group. Challenge everyone to think about couples they could invite to the next session.

9. Session One sets the tone for the study by establishing friendly, honest interaction about the topic of conflict. This session will help couples recognize that the differences between people are inevitable sources of friction in any relationship. Rather than viewing all conflict as negative, couples will learn to discern the ways in which differences can help foster growth and understanding in each individual and in their marriage.

10. Start the session on time, even if everyone is not present. Briefly share a few positive feelings about leading this study:

- Express your interest in strengthening your own marriage and dealing positively with conflict.

- Admit that your marriage and method of managing conflict are not perfect.

- State that the concepts in this study have been helpful in your marriage.

- Recognize that various individuals or couples may have been reluctant to attend.

- Thank group members for their interest and willingness to participate.

Hand out the study guides if you have not already done so, and give a quick overview of this study. Don't be afraid to do a little selling here—people need to know how they are going to benefit personally. They also need to know where this course will take them, especially if they are apprehensive about being a part of this study.

Commentary

Here is additional information about various Blueprints questions. The numbers that follow correspond to the Blueprints questions of the same numbers in the session. If you share any of these points, be sure to do so in a manner that does not stifle discussion by making you the authority with *the real answers*. Begin your comments by saying things like, "One thing I notice in this passage is…" or, "I think another reason for this is…"

Notes are not included for every question. Many of the questions in this study are designed for group members to draw from their own opinions and experiences.

1. Many people marry someone with a personality quite different from their own. A difference that is initially seen as an attractive quality may later be viewed as an irritant. There is a natural tendency for us to want and expect our spouse to act and think like we do.

2. A few major areas of potential disagreement are money management, child-rearing, and religion.

3. There are many answers to this question. For example, answers might include comments like, "Women may fail to realize how important work is to many men." "Men often fail to realize how much importance their wives place on the emotional side of a relationship.? "Men often forget how much women need regular, open communication." Encourage people to share out of their own experience, but remind them not to share anything that would embarrass their spouses.

4. This passage calls for us to not let anger and conflict go unresolved.

5. Unresolved conflict is like an infection that can plague a relationship for years. It builds walls of pain and bitterness that block communication and understanding.

9. These passages instruct us to pursue peace with others, and affirm that for peace to be real and lasting, it must come from God.

10. Peace from Christ is lasting and doesn't depend on circumstances. The peace that the world offers is temporary and superficial.

11. By receiving the forgiveness of sins and reconciliation Christ made possible by dying on the cross for our sin, we can experience peace with God.

12. God is the source of real peace and makes it available to his people.

Attention HomeBuilders Leaders

FamilyLife invites you to register your HomeBuilders group. Your registration connects you to the HomeBuilders Leadership Network, a worldwide movement of couples who are using HomeBuilders to strengthen marriages and families in their communities. You'll receive the latest news about HomeBuilders and other ministry opportunities to help strengthen marriages and families in your community. As the HomeBuilders Leadership Network grows, we will offer additional resources such as online training, prayer requests, and chat with authors. There is no cost or obligation to register; simply go to www.homebuildersgroup.com.

Session Two:

Transparency

Objectives

Resolving conflict in marriage requires transparency between you and your spouse.

In this session, couples will...

- look at what transparency is.

- examine the benefits of transparency in a relationship.

- discuss methods to improve transparency in their communication.

Notes and Tips

1. For the Warm-Up exercise in this session, couples will experience communicating with each other using three different "communication filters:" 1) clear (plastic wrap); 2) less clear (tissue); 3) obscured (a piece of paper). Give each couple one filter (plastic wrap, tissue, or paper). As couples are sharing about the kind of day they've had, call "time" after 30 seconds or so, and have couples trade filters with another couple and then resume their conversation. Do this a couple of times so that each couple experiences communicating using the three different filters. This exercise will illustrate the topic of transparency in a memorable way.

2. This is the second session, and your group members have probably warmed up a bit to each other. But they may not yet feel free to be completely open and honest about their relationship. Don't force the issue. Continue to encourage couples to attend and to complete their projects.

3. If someone joins the group for the first time in this session, give a brief summary of the main points of Session One. Also, be sure to introduce people who do not know each other. Also, consider giving new couples the chance to tell when and where they met.

4. Make sure the arrangements for refreshments (if you plan to have them) are covered.

5. If your group has decided to use a prayer list, make sure this is covered.

6. If you told the group during the first session that you'd ask them to relate something they learned from the first HomeBuilders Project, be sure to ask them. This is an important time for you to establish an environment of accountability.

7. For the closing prayer in this session, you may want to ask for a volunteer or two to close the group in prayer. Check ahead of time with a couple of people who you think might be comfortable praying aloud.

Commentary

Note: The numbers that follow correspond to the Blueprints questions of the same numbers in the session.

1. Suggest these words if your group doesn't come up with something similar: openness, honesty, and trust.

2. Factors may include a fear of rejection, an introverted personality, or growing up in an environment where transparency wasn't practiced.

3. The hope for transparency in marriage in damaged by things like criticism and busyness.

Transparency is needed because success in a marriage is more than just peaceful coexistence. Two people sharing and growing as individuals—and as a couple—is the goal toward which God intends us to strive.

7. In relation to Step Two, mention that although the important topic of forgiveness is only briefly mentioned here, an entire session later in the study is devoted to it because forgiveness is so important in relationships.

8. Affirmation increases your spouse's confidence and leads to a willingness to be transparent.

9. Honest prayer helps keep you humble toward God and toward each other.

Session Three:
Listening

Objectives

Conflict resolution requires a commitment to listen.

In this session, couples will...

- evaluate the listening habits of a couple in a case study.

- identify good and bad listening habits.

- select and practice several good listening habits.

Notes and Tips

1. Congratulations! With the completion of this session, you will be halfway through this study. It's time for a checkup: How are you feeling? How is the group going? What has worked well so far? What things might you consider changing as you head into the second half?

2. For the Warm-Up in this session, you need to tell the group *not* to turn the page in their books until you give the word. For this exercise to work most effectively, it is best if group members don't realize they're going to create a second list.

"For Extra Impact" with this activity, have a distracting noise, such as a radio, playing in the background when couples first share lists. If you do this, turn off the noise when couples share their second lists.

3. Remember the importance of starting and ending your session on time.

4. As an example to the group, it is important that you and your spouse complete the HomeBuilders Project each session.

5. Greet people as they arrive. Share personal expressions of appreciation for people's participation and support in earlier sessions. Tell people of your appreciation for the opportunity to get to know them better. Start the session on time.

Commentary

Note: The numbers that follow correspond to the Blueprints questions of the same numbers in the session.

1. Mention the following observations only if your group has trouble coming up with responses: Brian is guilty of not really listening, and Linda is guilty of trying to force Brian to listen to her at a time when he is not willing to do so.

2. Conflict can spring up quickly if one spouse believes that the other spouse isn't listening to him or her.

3. Here are some ideas you can relate, but be careful not to use these at the expense of stifling the group's discussion.

Brian could have lovingly mentioned that he can't listen to two things at the same time. Perhaps he could suggest that they talk as soon as the game is over. Also, he needs to assure her that football is not first in his life, but rather that this game is important at this time.

Linda's best option would have been to pick another time for this conversation. She could have accepted the signs of

Brian's inattention without using them as ammunition against him. Instead of drawing him into dialogue, she drove him away from it.

8. Taking the time to really listen helps build trust between you and your spouse. It also makes your spouse feel important, and encourages openness in your relationship.

9. Listening regularly to God through the Word helps you to keep your heart soft and teachable.

Session Four:
Confronting

Objectives

Loving confrontation can help a relationship by offering a way to practice real love.

In this session, couples will...

- learn various styles that people utilize when they deal with conflict.

- describe their styles of dealing with conflicts.

- discuss steps for dealing with conflict in a loving manner.

Notes and Tips

1. This session presents a discussion of a significant aspect of marital happiness—the importance of dealing appropriately with disagreements. Problem situations, small and large, important and insignificant, can create havoc in a relationship. Confrontation, especially with family members or close friends, is risky business. However, it is important and necessary. This session will help equip couples with practical guidelines for reaching the goal of healthy conflict resolution.

2. For the Warm-Up exercise in this session, it is OK for more than one couple to choose the same scenarios.

3. By this time, group members should be getting more comfortable with each other. For prayer at the end of this session, you may want to give everyone an opportunity to pray by asking the group to finish a sentence that goes something like this: "Lord, I want to thank you for ..." Be sensitive to anyone who may not feel comfortable doing this.

4. Make some notes immediately after the meeting to help you evaluate how this session went. Ask yourself questions such as: Did everyone participate? Is there anyone I need to make a special effort to follow up with before the next session? Asking yourself questions such as these will help you stay focused.

5. You and your spouse may can write notes of thanks and encouragement to the couples in your group this week. Thank them for their commitment and contribution to the group, and let them know that you are praying for them. Make a point to pray for them as you write their note.

Commentary

4. As Adam and Eve withdrew from God, so too do many couples respond to each other when they face conflict. This reaction often shows itself through physical separation. For example, instead of staying put, facing your spouse, and dealing with a conflict, you choose to leave the room.

Note: The numbers that follow correspond to the Blueprints questions of the same numbers in the session.

5. In this case, Pilate yielded to the crowd. In marriage, doing something only because it's easier than the alternative—talking through a conflict—can result in exchanging temporary relief for long-lasting bitterness and a more intense conflict in the future.

6. Saul fought to win. He attempted to use anger and violence to get his way. In marriage, this pattern is destructive. You may bring about peace temporarily, but you will cause bitterness to grow in the heart of your spouse.

7. Jesus addresses Martha in a loving and truthful manner. We should seek to follow Christ's example.

8. If you do not look inward, you may approach a confrontation with the wrong spirit—a spirit of pride, rather than gentleness and love. Also, you need to make sure you are not guilty of the same problem you are confronting someone else about!

11. Speaking the truth in love means presenting truth with sensitivity and gentleness, with the goal of helping the other person. Truth without love can bruise a person if it is told harshly or used as a weapon. If you love without truth, you may never confront that person because you're too afraid of hurting him or her. The person who needs to hear the truth is robbed of a chance to grow, and small issues can grow into large ones because they are never resolved.

Session Five:
Forgiving

Objectives

For peace to replace conflict, husband and wife must take responsibility to forgive each other.

In this session, couples will...

- learn how God's forgiveness is a model for us.

- study what is involved in seeking forgiveness.

- identify steps in forgiving and how they can implement these steps in their marriage.

Notes and Tips

1. In this session, you deal with the subject of forgiving. It might be wise to remind the group not to share anything that would embarrass their spouse.

2. If you believe that some people in your group may be struggling with the issue of forgiveness, mention the article in the back of their books, "Our Problems, God's Answers." They can read it on their own and may find it helpful.

3. One of the best things you can do for your group is to pray specifically for each group member. Why not take some time to pray as you prepare for this session?

4. For Wrap-Up in this session, instruct group members to jot down some responses to the case study before they discuss the questions.

5. *Looking ahead:* For the next session—the last session of this study—you may want to have someone, or a couple, describe what this study or group has meant to them. If this is something you would like to do, think about whom you will ask to share.

Commentary

Note: The numbers that follow correspond to the Blueprints questions of the same numbers in the session.

3. It is possible for us to experience forgiveness because of what God has done for us.

6. The prodigal son took responsibility for his actions, stated his error, asked his father to forgive him, and was willing to change his behavior and make restitution.

7. Forgiveness is cheapened if the person seeking forgiveness does not follow the steps outlined previously. Without these actions, a person may end up asking forgiveness for the same type of offenses over and over.

10. We are to set aside our angry feelings. We are not to seek revenge. We should not withhold forgiveness in order to "get even" or make someone suffer.

11. The Holy Spirit provides the power for you to do something that you may feel unable to do.

12. If your spouse is repentant and asks forgiveness, it is important not to hold past offenses against him or her.

Session Six:
A Blessing for an Insult

Objectives

People naturally tend to respond to hurts with anger. God promises to help us exchange these natural reactions for supernatural responses.

In this session, couples will...

- examine what insults and blessings are and how they affect a relationship.

- discuss the steps involved in establishing a "blessing" relationship.

- reflect on and evaluate their experience with this course.

Notes and Tips

1. This HomeBuilders Couples Series has great value, but people are likely to return to previous patterns of living unless they commit to a plan for continuing the progress they've made. During this final session of the course, encourage couples to take specific steps beyond this series to keep their marriages growing. For example, challenge couples who have developed the habit of a "date night" during this study to continue this practice. Also, you may want the group to consider doing another study from this series.

2. As a part of the last session, consider devoting some time to plan for one more meeting—a party to celebrate the completion of this study!

3. Session Six is perhaps the most practical of these sessions. Life is lived in the insult arena, whether the insults are subtle or open verbal war. Far too many conflicts escalate to volatile levels, not because the original problem was so crucial, but because things were said or done in haste and anger, making matters even more difficult to resolve. This session deals directly with our innate tendency to strike back when offended and shows how God offers a much better alternative: a blessing instead of an insult.

4. Greet people as they arrive. Comment about how time has flown and that your last session seems to have arrived so quickly. Begin planting anticipation for another study sometime in the future. Start the session on time.

Commentary

Note: The numbers that follow correspond to the Blueprints questions of the same numbers in the session.

1. The insult-for-insult relationship is defined as "meaning to hurt by remark or action." A person is hurt, so he wants to get even, saying in essence, "What you did hurt me, so I am going to hurt you." This type of relationship is rooted in an unforgiving and hardened heart. Selfishness is at its core.

2. Jesus entrusted himself "to him who judges justly." You may also want to reference Jesus' words found in Matthew 5:38-44.

5. The blessing-for-insult relationship can be defined as "continual active kindness." It is rooted in a forgiving and gracious heart. It means that when your spouse disappoints you or hurts you, your responsibility is to find a way to bless him or her. Giving a blessing means your hope is in God and his Word, and you choose to do good to another regardless of what has been done to you.

8. Prepare to give a practical example or two of demonstrated "blessing" from your marriage. Perhaps your spouse praised you in public or salvaged a bad situation by responding with love instead of anger. The responses to this question are key to group members' understanding of the principle of blessing and their ability to apply the principle in their marriages.

9. Most insults are verbal. If you can control your tongue, you'll probably eliminate most of your insults. However, this is no small task (see James 3:1-8).

10. Before you act, force yourself to think through your alternatives instead of reacting. You have to deliberately choose not to respond to an insult with wrong motives.

112303

Recommended Reading

Achieving the Impossible: Intimate Marriage, Charles M. Sell

The Blessing, Gary Smalley and John Trent

Caring Enough to Confront, David Augsburger

Caring Enough to Forgive, David Augsburger

Communication: Key to Your Marriage, H. Norman Wright

Dr. Rosberg's Do-It-Yourself Relationship Mender,
    Gary Rosberg

How Can It Be All Right When Everything Is All Wrong?
    Lewis B. Smedes

How to Experience God's Love and Forgiveness, Bill Bright

Love Life for Every Married Couple, Ed Wheat

The New Building Your Mate's Self-Esteem, Dennis and
    Barbara Rainey

The Secret of Staying in Love, John Powell

Staying Close, Dennis Rainey

To Understand Each Other, Paul Tournier